ISBN-13:   978-1501048586
ISBN-10:   1501048589

LCCN: 2014922195

Printed in South Carolina, USA

Introduction

What inspired us to write *Beyond the Book ~How to Start or Jumpstart a Book Club?*

We love reading an exceptional book, transporting ourselves to another time, place or era. Dreaming big, we wonder where the next novel will take us. Its characters add literary flavor, making for a compelling night in with drama, love, laughter, compassion, intrigue and, yes, sometimes even outrage.

We have been members of the same book club for more than a decade and have become experts on the subject. What initially began with four members has, over time, become a dedicated and enthusiastic group of seven who have formed lasting friendships. We celebrate each other's successes and are there for each other during times of great loss and difficulty.

When you experience something that has enriched your life, you want to tell the world. It can be likened to winning the lottery – too cool to keep secret. The advice in this book comes from our own book club experiences – we know what worked for us and what did not. We offer our best-tested ideas, some entertaining tips, and helpful checklists throughout these pages.

Our goal is to inspire others to follow our lead and start a club of their own (or add flare and spark into their existing club). To do that, all you really need is this book and your book-loving reading buddies and you are ready to go! Your association may forge lasting bonds, taking your membership to more than just a book club – going well Beyond the Book!

Suzanne Colley

Kathleen Marsan

You will see this icon throughout this book alongside personalized guidance. All combined, we offer something for every book club lover out there and we hope to help you on the path to creating (or jumpstarting) your own book club!

Table of Contents

"To accomplish great things, we must not only act, but also dream; not only plan, but believe."

~ Anatole France

Chapter 1:

Why Start a Book Club

For the book lover, membership in a book club can provide a forum to share reading as a much-loved activity.

Book club discussions are educational and thought provoking. It is amazing the number of opinions people have on any given plot. There is always plenty to discuss whether the book is loved or not, or judged to be somewhere in between.

From humor, to romance, or to the more serious theme, a book club can explore all genres with great enthusiasm. Any category works – memoir, mystery, drama, adventure, or biography the list never ends. Your club can specialize by reading only non-fiction or can branch out and explore all facets of literature.

There are three precepts to book club membership:

- Socialization / *get yourself out there*
- Entertainment / *the best pastime ever*
- Education / *knowledge can be gained from every book*

To help determine if starting a book club is for you, ask yourself: Do you . . .

- Spend most of your free time in bookstores?

- Scan the bestseller list weekly?

- Read until you are bleary-eyed?

- Read to escape reality?

- Have more books than bookshelves?

- Have more bookmarks than credit cards?

- Discuss your latest read with anyone who will listen?

- Still worship your seventh grade literature teacher?

- Find yourself in line at midnight waiting for the latest book release?

- Go to book signings?

- Dress up for Halloween as literary characters?

    Did you name your child or pet after favorite authors?

- Always have a novel on hand should you catch a quiet moment?

- Like to savor a book and take your time reading at night or on rainy days?

- Start your conversations with: "Did you read..?" "What did you think about that book..?" "Have you read any of..?" or "What have you read lately?"

If you answered "yes" to any (or all) of these questions, starting a book club is for you and this book is a must read!

When you start a book club, you inspire yourself and others to set aside time for reading and you help others move past the excuses such as "I might read that book someday when I have time." Your club can motivate others to embrace reading and start using phrases such as "I cannot wait to get my hands around that book!"

Need more reasons to start or join a book club?

Keep your mind active, develop yourself as a person, network, de-stress, fulfill the dream of always wanting to be in a book club.

Enjoy the company of likeminded folks, make new friends, stay active, enjoy a night out, pursue an inexpensive hobby, get to know your neighbors.

Share an interest, swap books among friends, fulfill your bucket list, entertain and be entertained, talk about books, enjoy intellectual discussions, share a love of avid reading.

Chapter 2

Building Your Book Club ~ Getting the Chemistry Right

Now that you have decided to start a club of your own, the next step is to find others who share this common interest. Your initial investment of time and energy to formulate the group is crucial for success and longevity. This chapter offers an effective method toward recognizing potential members, and building a great book club. Use it as a guide to creating or boosting your unique book club!

When, What, Where, Why and Who

Think about **when** you first had the idea to start a book club? Were you a guest at a friend's group? Did you read an article extolling the virtues of starting a club of your own? Numerous magazine articles and television hosts gush over how much fun it is to be in a book club. Was that the catalyst to begin the process? Was it due to seeing this book on the shelf that got you thinking? Your honest assessment will guide you to the type of club you hope to create.

Envision yourself surrounded by other booklovers. **What** characteristics will define your club?

You would not drive a car without a solid chassis, or build a house without a firm foundation. The same theory applies towards developing your book club. Start with the basics.

- Should the club be serious in nature or lighthearted and free-flowing?

- Should members be of the same gender or occupation, or will you create an eclectic group?

- Will the group be venturesome adding special field trips and themes to the mix?

- Will your literary material be exclusive or inclusive?

All historical fiction, autobiographies, or mysteries club

- What about the meeting schedule?

Time, place, frequency

- What about the meeting location?

Consistent or a variety of settings

8

Where do you wish to go with your club? Question yourself: What is your comfort level? Is it with conquering voluminous tomes and offering complicated expositions, or simply making critiques among cohorts?

Why do so much thinking and planning? Longevity and maintaining membership should be your goal. As the founder of a book club, you provide a social as well as an educational environment. So, lay a strong foundation from which all your best ideas will emerge and grow.

As your club develops and other people hear of how great your group is, they may ask if they can join – and that is the definitive compliment.

Who would you like to invite to join your book club? Are you bringing together people that complement one another, and that inspire new ideas and stimulate the conversation? Since this will become the essence of the club, getting the chemistry right is essential.

Consider the people you discuss novels or share paperbacks with – are they always anxious to compare notes? Do you recommend a read to your best friend, who in turn recommends it to her friend? These are natural, organic ways to start a book club – and you are the guiding force on this literary adventure!

Finding Members

How *do* you find members? Putting together a book club is not much different from working on a first-rate puzzle. You could look near, tapping into those you already know, or you could look far by advertising in the newspaper, the community bulletin board at your local library, or by posting a sign at work.

If you are not sure how you would put together a club, attend a club already in existence (at a library or book store). Take note of how the dynamics fall into place and what works well. Another approach is to find a book-loving friend to meet and discuss a club concept. Start by each recommending one member to join; then using this method, add to your group.

With any approach, use our Personality Checklist as a guide to uncovering hidden jewels and red flags that may be lurking in your potential members.

You may experience periods of trial and error when first putting together your own book club. Do not despair – that is the beauty of the evolution.

Remember those **when, what, where, why and who** questions you asked yourself earlier in this chapter and work within those parameters to find the right mix of people who will be contributing to the dialog.

When all is said and done ~ the clever insights, the lively conversations, and the pleasure derived from your meetings together ~ you will know that the chemistry is right. Stay positive and relish in the excitement of forming a successful book club.

Personality Checklist

We put together this mock list for you to examine; note our hidden jewels as well as red flags! This summary personifies an imaginary book club. The examples listed are fictitious, but the concept works.

Potential Members	Personalities	Reason for Inviting
Kate Allegro	Very active volunteer, loves the arts, enjoys new challenges	Avid reader, gregarious, very enthusiastic
Suzy Richard	Intellectual, adventurous	Recommends interesting reads
Lisa Rhodes	Liberal, magnetic personality, good conversationalist	Loves unusual books, frequents bookstores
Esther Smith	Very shy, likeable	Only reads Harlequins
Abby Grant	Opinionated, boisterous, spirited, knowledgeable	Voracious reader, very entertaining
Kirstin Williams	Sweet, very talkative, loves to read	Works in a bookstore, good friend of Esther and encourages her to expand her choice of books
Becca Taylor	Opinionated, Type A personality	Abby's acquaintance, she is Kate's neighbor and never agrees with anything Kate says
Ruth Harris	Kind and considerate	Devoted reader, might enjoy hosting meetings
Gerard Miller	Outspoken; watches book discussions on television	Reads bestsellers, mysteries, Louis L'Amour, expressed an interest in joining a book club.
Cindy Gagnon	Organized, is in several book clubs and wants to help organize this one	Good resource person, will keep the discussion flowing

Looking at this list, most of the personalities would make great potential members; some need further review.

11

- Esther Smith is a good candidate even though she is limited in the style of books she likes, but according to her friend Kirstin, Esther is willing to try new ideas.

- Although Abby is very opinionated, her strength is energizing stimulating conversation and encouraging others to join in the discussions.

- Becca is definitely not someone you would want monopolizing the discussions or disrespecting any member's opinion. We would invite Abby Grant instead of Becca.

- Gerard may be uncomfortable being the only male, but he is still a good consideration for the group. Invite him to give it a try.

Now start on your own potential membership list.

*Participation equals
responsibility, commitment and
book club personality.*

Chapter 3

Selecting Your Books

The selection process of what to read is the heart of a book club. It is the compelling force that draws your membership to meetings, and sparks lively conversation. There are several ways to research your choice of book selections by using resources right at your fingertips, including:

- **Club members** – Encourage members to research and recommend multiple book options. This is a sure way for all members to discover books they may not have otherwise selected, and to arrive at a variety of reads while keeping the selection process fun and interesting.

- **Other book clubs** – When the opportunity presents itself to be with or network with members of other book clubs, accept it – and listen for reading suggestions. In general, if one club is excited about a book, your group may share that same enthusiasm. Interests vary widely among groups. Keep a file of their recommendations and refer to them when making future picks. Track information such as: What is the title? Who is the author? What was the book about and did it promote discussion?

- **Co-workers** – Most likely, there are more than a few avid readers tucked away at your work place. The next time you are in the cafeteria to pour a cup of coffee, check out those around you who might be caught up in the pages while away from their "in-box" routine. When

15

they close the cover or come up for a look-around, go ahead confirm this mutual pastime, ask about that particular book. Capitalize on the possibility that you share common author interest. Do not miss the opportunity to solicit the next "best read ever."

- **Libraries** – Book clubs are popular throughout the nation and many libraries host their own formal dialogues. Communities in conjunction with their libraries offer town wide book discussions with authors making guest appearances. Look into these types of events for reading suggestions and tips on running a book club.

  In addition to our monthly meeting, our group often attends the library's Town Wide Reading program together.

- **Book stores** – *Authors, volumes, and pages, oh my*! Take the time to browse the bookshelves and book stores large and small! Quite often store employees are willing to share their favorites and many bookstores post employees' "pick of the week." Look for displays that draw attention to special events such as author appearances. Go ahead, judge a book by its cover. Read the jacket, go deeper, browse a few pages – you may uncover a "best pick."

- **The media** – Pick up any newspaper or magazine and you are bound to find a book suggestion or review offered. Historically, the New York Times bestseller list is a widely used source and is often posted in libraries and book stores. Look in your local newspaper for current articles or reviews.

Many television and radio talk show programs often highlight guest authors and feature their work. For your reading appetite, explore these programs and their websites for recaps and details.

- **Movies based on books** – Producers and directors often recognize the enormous potential of a good book by bringing it to the screen where the narrative springs to life and the characters leap from the pages. You may want to select books you know are being made into movies for your club to read.

- **The Internet** – Boundless possibilities exist within this search vehicle to explore book reviews, hone in on a specific genre, or read author's profiles. Once your research is complete, the ultimate opportunity awaits you to purchase books or download an e-book to your Kindle®, iPad®, etc. (Check out www.half.com, www.amazon.com for starters.)

- **Reach back to your own past** – Take a second look at the classics you read in high school or college – and take a look at the lists being used in schools today. It may be a fascinating comparison in retrospect. Additionally remember that educators are a great resource and have a propensity to share information. You may even want to consider reconnecting with your favorite teacher for his or her suggestions.

Explore reading outside of your comfort zone; even a dud has something to offer (although you may discern that you won't attempt that author again).

17

*Of course, read the
book first then compare
it to the movie.*

Chapter 4

Establishing the Meeting Location and Time

In order to achieve full participation from your club members, it is necessary to establish a meeting location and time that is suitable to everyone. Setting (and keeping) an established meeting time and place eliminates confusion. This may seem like a daunting task but *trust us*, unanimous agreement is possible.

Although you may have a preconceived idea about where and when your group should meet, dedicate a portion of your introductory meeting to working out all meeting details. This is the time to give thought to and exchange ideas as to what your group prefers. Should your group decide on alternating times or locations, just be sure a scribe keeps everyone informed.

While the options for a meeting place are numerous, consider these potential locations.

- **A club member's home** – The home is often a comfortable environment and its shelter allows for conversation that is more intimate. By hosting at home, each member has the opportunity to incorporate his or her own personality into the gathering whether it happens to take place around the kitchen table, on the deck, or seated on comfy couches.

Hosting Tip

Always remind your family when book club is coming over and always label food and drink meant for the club. One time our host spent hours making chocolate candy for the book club meeting. Unfortunately, it was gobbled up by her unsuspecting family earlier that day.

- **Tea/coffeehouse** – These "ready for you" locations foster a stress-free laidback atmosphere.

- **Restaurants** – Dining out provides that "catered to" feeling and can be on any scale; breakfast, dinner or just a beverage with dessert. Here you can relax and have someone else pour that second cup of coffee.

- **Book stores** – Surround yourselves with what you *love* . . . books, books and more books. Having your meetings at these larger venues affords not only a discussion platform but, the chance to shop for future picks. As a bonus, you might even catch a noteworthy or budding author featuring their latest release.

20

Smaller new and used bookstores might be diamonds in the rough; do not overlook these interesting prospects.

- **Libraries** – Most libraries offer private or semi-private rooms for meetings and are usually at no cost. Do not forget to take your confirmation receipt with you on the night of the meeting just in case someone is using the room you reserved.

- **Alternative settings** – Relating your latest read to a local site that corresponds to the storyline gives your club license to venture out and discover perhaps an uncharted local gem. Keeping the location relevant to your selection will set the stage and fuel the discussion.

  For "off-site" meeting locations, it is prudent and sometimes required to make reservations. We recommend visiting the location site ahead of time for a preview.

- The following examples show how a club might establish its meeting location and time:

21

Example A

Title	*Author*	*Date*	*Host/Location**	*Time*
Girl with the Pearl Earring	Tracy Chevalier	1/21	Kate Allegro	7:00 PM
Share your favorite poem night	You choose the Poet	2/18	Esther Smith	7:00 PM
The Alchemist	Paulo Coelho	3/18	Ruth Harris	7:00 PM
The Worst Hard Time	Timothy Egan	4/15	Suzy Richard	7:00 PM
Blue Diary	Alice Hoffman	5/20	Cindy Gagnon	7:00 PM
Longitude	Dava Sobel	6/10	Rhode Island (overnight) Suzy Richard	10:00 AM
The Devil and the White City	Erik Larson	7/12	Abby Grant	7:00 PM
Red Tent	Anita Diamant	8/19	Book Store Kate Allegro	1:00 PM
Kite Runner	Khaled Hosseini	9/16	Kirstin Williams	7:00 PM
Midnight in the Garden of Good and Evil	John Berendt	10/22	Tea party at an historical locale Esther Smith	10:00 AM
To Kill a Mocking Bird	Harper Lee	11/4	Cindy Gagnon	7:00 PM
Pope Joan	Donna Woolfolk Cross	12/15	Holiday Celebration Gerard Miller	7:00 PM

Notes to members: Town Wide Read *on April 7 - Highlighted Author: Andrew Gross; Make reservations with Cindy.*
Two-way Tie - *Pick your favorite for the 13th book: Dog On It by Spencer Quinn or The Heretic's Daughter by Kathleen Kent. Both slated for summer discussion.*
Reminder: *Active participation includes hosting, book suggestions, selection, field trip planning, and payment of dues.*
All meetings are at the host's home unless otherwise specified.

Example B

Title	Author	Date	Host/Location*	Time
Bliss Remembered	Frank DeFord	1/23	Ruth Harris	7:00 PM
Triangle	David Vondrehle	2/19	Gerard Miller	7:00 PM
Swan Thieves	Elizabeth Kostova	3/19	Kate Allegro	7:00 PM
Curious Incident of the Dog in the Nightime	Mark Haddon	4/16	Cindy Gagnon	7:00 PM
I am Murdered	Bruce Chadwick	5/8	Coffee Shop Kirstin Williams	7:00 PM
Fatal Forecast	Michael J. Tougias	6/18	RI (overnight) Suzy Richard	10:00 AM
The Alienist	Caleb Carr	7/24	Lisa Rhodes	7:00 PM
Sacred Cows	Karen E. Olsen	8/15	Esther Smith	7:00 PM
The Next Thing on My List	Jill Smolonski	9/17	Abby Grant	7:00 PM
Little Bee	Chris Cleave	10/27	Kirstin Williams	10:00 AM
Gargoyle	Andrew Davidson	11/19	Suzy Richard	7:00 PM
Into Thin Air	John Krakauer	12/5	Restaurant (holiday) Abby Grant	7:00 PM

Notes to members: Special Meeting: 8/15, visit by noted author Karen E. Olsen. Bring your copy of her book, Sacred Cows, for signing.
Reminder: *Active participation includes hosting, book suggestions, selection, field trip planning, and payment of dues.*
All meetings are at the host's home unless otherwise specified.

Why establish book club standards and guidelines?

Despite all good ground rules, a bit of discord may still arise. This chapter presents some of our proven ways to best handle tricky challenges. Of course, we cannot address all human foibles... but we hope this is helpful just the same!

Chapter 5

Book Club Etiquette

Whether your book club is brand new or has been in existence for a while, good manners matter. In this chapter, we offer guidelines on how to keep your book club running smoothly, and should discord arise, how to deal with it effectively. We will discuss the basic guidelines, which include a standard of book club etiquette and rules for maintaining your club's credo. These instructions are tantamount to well attended, successful and energetic meetings.

In order to potentially head off future unpleasant dealings, introduce the subject of "rules" or a "code of conduct" at the time of your group's formation. We realize this can be a tricky topic.

Plan for an organizational discussion early on so members can agree upon – and fully acknowledge – the club's rules/codes. These guidelines will set the tone and provide helpful tools for future predicament resolution– and play a part in the overall success of your club. First, you should determine the following:

Leadership – Will your group have an assigned leader, spokesperson, or facilitator to provide a level of stability and consistency? This leadership role can be permanent or rotated among members.

Membership – Will you cap membership? Can members request to be on an inactive list? How long will it be maintained? Will you dismiss members who do not follow rules and participate? Or, will you institute resolutions based on your rules?

For the existing club, it is never too late to establish rules, standards, and guidelines. Plan a meeting think-tank session just to focus on rules. Our club meets once a year to review, reconnect, and re-evaluate our guidelines.

Enforcement – Will your group establish consequences for non-adherence and a process by which the guidelines are to be enforced?

Once you institute standards for your club, commit to them. If your club is opposed to creating a formal doctrine, encourage your members instead to define what is acceptable.

Incorporating guiding principles is necessary for any club, and a book club is no exception.

Next, consider basic etiquette standards for your book club. We suggest the following:

- **Respect each other's opinions** – There is no wrong conclusion about a book; it is an individual assessment. There will always be different outlooks surrounding a novel, and frankly, without it there would be no need for dialog. Enjoy the myriad of personal insights and thoughts as each add texture and scope to your discourse. Passion on either side of a book's value is essential ~ draw from the diversity of thought. Members should feel free to speak openly and without fear of reproach.

- **Do not monopolize the conversation** – Once you have contributed your own views, sit back, and relax. Participation on your part does not give way to a monopoly.

- **Do not interrupt** – Banter is fine until it shuts someone down. All members deserve a chance to complete a thought.

- **Recognize each other's sensitivities** – Be aware of other's perspectives. Unless your club has agreed to read and discuss the more controversial topics, be cognizant of its subject matter when your group selects a book.

- **Read the book** – Whatever the selection, and even if the going gets tough, read on. Imagine coming to the meeting ready to impart your insights only to discover you are the sole conversant. Do not come just for "general chatter." *Give the book – and your club – its due!*

- **Focus on the book** – Conversational straying may indicate your group's dialogue needs some prodding. The host for the meeting can pre-plan questions, a tactic to help members stay focused on the discussion. Should your club continue to have difficulty staying on topic or if the discussion lacks energy, have a facilitator or designee directed discussion.

- **Other scenarios to consider when drafting guidelines**

  o **Unannounced guests -** Unless your group has an "open-door" policy, it is courteous to give advanced notice to all members of a potential guest.

  o **Rude, flippant or crude language -** Although sometimes culturally acceptable, your group may decide to leave it at the door!

  o **Worst book ever -** So you picked a dud; it happens. Remember, it's the book that has a problem, not you. Remind members that negative comments about the book are no reflection on any member.

  A note from Suzanne: Our group sometimes cringes when I recommend an offbeat or unusual selection. That has never stopped me from exploring new authors and bringing them to the group's attention!

Welcoming New Members

When your group welcomes a new member, have them come to a meeting prior to officially joining. This introduction process works because it takes the pressure off the "newbie," allowing them to experience club dynamics, how the meeting flows, and how members interact. While this is a great time to review rules and expectations the club has from each member, it is also a great time to reminisce. Take some time to review your club's history with the new member and share a few highlights (which member joined when, what the first book was for the club, highlights from field trips and other great meeting venues, etc.).

Handling Tough Situations with Members

The following chart illustrates a few possible member challenges – along with a quick look at how our club recommends handling them:

	SCENARIO:	SUGGESTION:	NOTES:
Maury Monopolize	Maury is well read and loves to expound upon whatever topic is under discussion. In keeping with his routine, once he starts, there is little anyone can do to stop him. His behavior prevents others from participating, thereby annoying members.	The facilitator or designee can easily handle this situation by taking Maury aside and assuring him that he is an asset to the club. Remind him the meeting calls for group participation and he needs to allow everyone a turn at expressing opinion.	*The facilitator or designee has the opportunity to guide the more outspoken member to "wait their turn" and encourage other members an opportunity to articulate.*
Nina NoComment	Nina comes to every meeting and seems to enjoy the socialization aspect, yet rarely contributes to the book discussion. In fact, the majority of the time she has not even cracked the book's binding. Nina is your classic undedicated reader. Members are confused – why is Nina in a *book club*?	Your club may feel it is just fine for Nina to sit quietly and enjoy an evening out. Or, you may insist on active participation in the discussion – which may be a higher level of participation than Nina seems willing to give. It is time to remind her of that fundamental precept . . . *she is in a book club!*	*Think of Nina's interest as a compliment to your club and its membership. In this scenario, it might make most sense for Nina to host a social gathering for the group in lieu of coming to meetings.*
Kurt Curt	Since joining the club, Kurt has been late for every meeting; and is loud, disruptive, and ultra-opinionated. His approach makes others uncomfortable and his vehement insistence that his interpretation is the only correct one causes others anxiety.	Explain to Kurt why his demeanor is unacceptable and why because of it, he can no longer be a member of the group. If a person clearly does not fit in, for the good of the membership, there may only be one solution – dismissal.	*In this, an uncomfortable situation, you can be thankful for your club's etiquette and behavior agreement that lets you act judiciously and authoritatively. Don't be confrontational, but do remind everyone that membership guidelines call for responsibility to the entire group!*

Arthur Allaboutme	Arthur is gregarious, always reads the book, and loves to share his general life experiences in relation to the book. Recently, he has experienced some *very* private trials; and he now uses the club meeting as group therapy. Everyone is impatient and tired of hearing about his extremely personal plights rather than his insights about the latest selection.	The facilitator or another member should take Arthur aside and assure him that everyone sympathize with his concerns. Be earnest and remind him that a book discussion meeting is an inappropriate forum for sharing his most intimate problems – and encourage him to share his personal affairs outside of the club setting. Remind him how much his contribution about the novel is of value to the meeting.	*Arthur may feel hurt and decide to walk out or perhaps even quit the club. When addressing member's concerns such as this scenario, that is an inherent risk. Be compassionate and discrete, yet firm.*
Debbie Doesn't-Fit	When Debbie first joined the group, she was an active participant and seemed to be enjoying the meetings. Recently her level of contribution has dwindled and she mentioned to a few members that she is looking into joining a different book club.	Don't take it personally. Debbie will be happier and more productive when she finds the right book club fit. This is not a personal affront to your particular group rather a matter of her individual preference.	*Address the issue of "when a member leaves the group" in your club's guidelines. Your club cannot be all things to all people, so relax and wish those who move on the best of luck.*

So you can see why having an established set of rules for your book club is so very helpful. Guidelines (along with respect, patience, and commonsense) give members the ability to address almost any situation with greater certainty and influence – and helps set up your club for long-term success.

31

Participation is critical to success. Discussing your group's needs and expectations will prevent disappointment later. Keep a phone/email list of all members to communicate any unforeseen schedule changes.

Chapter 6

Incorporating Themes into Meetings
Go Beyond the Binder!

It should not matter if your group meets in a public setting or in a member's home. Incorporating themes can be easy.

Think back on your favorite parties. What was it about them that stood out? In all likelihood, someone took the time to create an interesting atmosphere for his or her guests. The host's care and effort created a noteworthy and memorable experience. This same consideration inspires the book club host to decorate with a bookish flare.

Adding a theme to your meeting does wonders to stimulate conversation. Inspired by your latest read, incorporating themes into your club meeting can create that added touch to take your meetings to a new level.

Themed book discussion is more than just a pretty table; it inspires and motivates the participant. Become your group's raconteur, spinner of yarns, and teller of tales, by creating a dynamic meeting.

Using Themes

The rule with themes is that there are no rules. Themes breathe new life into meetings while making the characters, settings, and subject matter three-dimensional.

The first step to selecting a theme is to review the book and think back on its nuances. Then, ask yourself:

- What stood out?

- What do you recall about a character or setting?

- What was symbolic in the book?

- What chapters do you want to highlight?

- What inspired the theme?

- What impression do you intend to impart on your members?

Our club members often select their host night by the theme possibilities it presents.

Four Basics to Theme Building

1. **Brainstorm** – Jot down ideas and random thoughts. The sky is the limit at this point, but in the end, keep it realistic.

2. **Plan** – Once the theme is set and musings become a practicality, create the meeting and plan for a book-inspired dialogue. Prepare discussion questions, organize decorations, and create a list of "what to do" and "when to do it."

3. **Shop** – After your plan is in place, make a list of what items you need (food, beverages, decorations, props, etc.) and how much is required. Seek out your local party store, dollar store or thrift shop for unlimited embellishment possibilities. These can range from wacky to refined, low-cost to expensive. It is all up to your imagination.

4. **Meeting night** – To prevent frustration and stress, allow plenty of time for set up (we cannot stress this enough!). Sure, that sounds easy; but trust us on this. Thinking that a task takes 10 minutes only to find out it is more like half an hour can fluster the steadiest of hosts. Set the table, arrange your props and prepare snacks and beverages ahead of time, have your teapot almost whistling, and coffee pot percolating. Greet your guests with a smile and enjoy the meeting.

Preplanning works, remember you set the tone! So, relax, let the book and your theme be the motivation for a great book club!

Themes Based Upon the Book or its Genre

Our members enjoy meetings with a theme. The following illustrates a few of our favorites:

- In Michelle Moran's book *Cleopatra's Daughter,* the main character was born to royalty and should have lived her life dressed in rich, exotically woven, free-flowing fabrics. Fate turned her life upside down; yet in spite of the betrayal, deceit, murder and mayhem, she regained an empire and empowered a country's citizens. Our book club host treated us as crowned heads by setting a table that would please a queen and her king. Delicious grapes, aged wine, and an array of fabulous trinkets displayed on a silver platter enticed lively discourse on the lifestyle of the Roman Empire and its rich and famous.

- *Fried Green Tomatoes at the Whistle Stop Café* by Fannie Flagg was an extraordinary tale of the unique bonds of friendship and love, coming of age, and finding one's purpose in life. This novel offered our club a variety of hosting and creative theme ideas. Our host requested each person recreate a signature dish from the book with the emphasis on the much-touted fried green tomatoes. After sampling the southern style dishes – which included chicken and dumplings, grilled pork, black eyed peas, bacon with green beans, fried corn, deviled eggs, sweet potato and pecan pie and of course, fried green tomatoes – we adjourned to the living room to watch "Fried Green Tomatoes," the movie version of the book. The discussion focused on the casting preferences and artistic interpretations between the author and the director of the movie.

It is easy to choose a theme based on a book that was made into a movie. From the drama of *To Kill a Mocking Bird* by Harper Lee to the exotic with subtitles such as The *Girl with the Dragon Tattoo* by Stieg Larsson, a group can pick from a whole range of drama, comedy, or historical fiction. Your theme can be as elaborate as ours was, or as simple as making it a movie night with popcorn, goodies, and light discussion.

Ramping up a Theme

Richard Zacks historical narrative, *The Pirate Hunter: The True story of Captain Kidd,* inspired our hostess to hoist the Jolly Roger outside her home. She greeted members dressed as a pirate, and further set the mood with swashbuckling pirate songs resounding in the background. The kitchen table was set with a treasure chest for each member filled with booty (candy and gold doubloons). Keeping with the theme, a co-conspirator brought a mechanical parrot that randomly interrupted conversations with pirate lingo and chants for crackers, thoroughly entertaining the group.

Prior to the meeting, our hostess searched for interesting facts on the internet and discovered an e-mail address for the author. In a quest for more information about the book, she contacted Mr. Zacks and asked his advice on discussion notes for our meeting. Much to our delight, he graciously responded and expressed his pleasant surprise that a women's book club chose to read *Pirate Hunter.*

Ironically, the week of our meeting, the news reporters were heralding the discovery of Captain Kidd's ship, the "Quedagh Merchant," by scuba diver archaeologist Charles Beeker. The ship had been resting at the bottom of the sea off the coast of the Catalina Islands in the Dominican Republic. This current event added to our timely dialog, making the night that much more interesting!

Motivating Conversation

All of the props and gadgets that you strategically place for your themed meeting are simply great conversation starters. If the discussion goes off-topic, a theme works wonders at bringing the crowd back around to the subject matter.

As an added twist, our hostess researched the history of women pirates and shared those findings. One can imagine the rousing conversation topics these infamous women evoked! The hostess also found a website with questions about New England pirates – which were printed, cut into strips, and placed in a "treasure chest" centerpiece. In game show format, each member pulled questions from the chest. The club member with the most correct answers won additional booty.

After reading *Water for Elephants* by Sara Gruen, our meeting host guided us back to our childhood memories of circus tents, ringmasters, clowns, tightrope acrobats, wild animals, and lest we forget ~ elephants. To invoke the magic of the arena, the table's centerpiece consisted of small stuffed animals, and authentic buckets filled with fresh popcorn. We enjoyed roasted peanuts in their shell, circus peanuts (yes, those silly orange yummies), and cotton candy. The emotions this theme provoked gave us all something unique to discuss. We recalled from the novel, Jacob's story of the difficulties that he encountered before and while traveling with the circus. Foremost in the discussion was how our own lives changed as we grew older. This book fast became an all-time favorite. The richness of this novel inspired each member to travel back in time, not only to reflect, but to think and plan for the future.

Thinking and developing a discussion strategy beforehand helps the meeting format (benefitting both host and participants). Here are some tried-and-true tips and queries for building great discussions:

- Ask open-ended questions about the book.

- If a book contains sensitive subject matter, keep your members' sensitivities in mind when determining how to approach that particular topic.

- While immersed in the genre of historical fiction, study the language. Did "facts" start as mere possibility in one paragraph and by the next become an absolute truth, blurring the lines between historical fiction and historical text? Reading historical fiction lends itself to some feisty discussion.

- Did a mystery intentionally lead you down the wrong path? Did you feel cheated by that tactic?

- Were members able to unravel the clues alongside the lead character?

- Did the readers delight in elaborate details from the author?

- Discuss readers' thoughts about how the novel was constructed (chronologically, using several points of view, going back in time, etc.). How did this affect the storyline?

- The ending of a book is just as important at what came before and can create lively discussions. Ask if club members prefer to have all the loose ends finalized before turning that final page. Do they prefer to leave the book's conclusion up to reader interpretation? Should the author leave room for a sequel?

Meeting Theme Worksheet

What follows is a sample from one of our member's worksheets which was used to plan a memorable themed book club meeting. We have also included a blank worksheet for you to use to help organize and create your own themed meetings.

The decision to use a theme can be incorporated at almost any point: when your group selects a book, when planning the meeting, when the mood strikes, or when an opportunity presents itself. You can give the host the freedom to choose a theme (or not), or you can predetermine "theme nights" and ask for volunteers.

Meeting Theme Worksheet

Meeting Date   **Title & Author**

___June 18___   *South of Broad, Pat Conroy*

Brainstorm:

A lot of choices for discussion – use questions in the back of the
book (or search the Internet for questions).
Lots of characters / each should be discussed in depth.
Each member will become a character based on the seat they pick.

Plan:

Write name of character on individual papers – to be placed into
small boxes.
Print out questions, cut into strips and place in community
container.

Shopping List:

Props: Find book shaped boxes at local art store (for character
names).
Food: Cheesecake variety platter / mixed nuts (symbolizing
diversity).
Drinks: Sweet tea with mint (northern spin).

Meeting Night:

Upon arrival, have members choose a seat; inform them not to
peek in the boxes. When ready, have members open boxes,
introduce themselves as their "character," stay in character
throughout the meeting. Each "character" picks a discussion
question from the community container.

Meeting Theme Worksheet

Meeting Date   **Title & Author**

_____   _____

Brainstorm:

_____

_____

_____

Plan:

_____

_____

_____

Shopping List:

_____

_____

_____

_____

Meeting Night:

_____

_____

_____

Checklist for Book Club Hosting

Use this list as a guide to organize and formulate a plan for hosting the book club. This checklist works for a large assembly or a small, intimate group (or anywhere in between), and is useful whether planned months, weeks, or days in advance.

Type of meeting:	Dietary considerations:	Two weeks before the meeting:
☐ Centered on the book's theme	☐ Vegetarian member(s): _____	☐ Send out invitations (electronic/email, phone, snail-mail) along with RSVP requests and directions to your home.
☐ Holiday (seasonal or specific such as St. Patrick's Day)	☐ Member(s) with food allergies (peanut, strawberry, milk, nuts, chocolate, or other):	☐ Make sure you have enough place settings for your guests.
☐ Non-theme meeting	_____	
	☐ Other dietary needs: _____	☐ Purchase paper goods.
Number of people expected: ____		
	Menu:	☐ Bake and freeze desserts or other foods that can be prepared ahead.
	☐ Hors d'oeuvre / finger foods	
	☐ Dinner	Take an inventory of the room in which the meeting will take place:
	☐ Dessert	
	☐ Coffee / tea / soda etc.	☐ Is seating adequate?
		☐ Is lighting suitable?
		☐ Enough places for members to set dishes and drinks?

One week before the meeting:	**Day before the meeting:**	**Shortly before the meeting:**
☐ If necessary, send out meeting reminders.	☐ Leave out coasters and / or put on tablecloths.	☐ Set the table or food serving area with glassware, cups, plates, etc.
☐ Shop for groceries and/or decorations (remind family members not to eat food meant for the book club!).	☐ Check the times for baking, cooking, or reheating. *Give yourself plenty of time for trial and error!*	☐ Put finger foods on platters in the refrigerator ready to go.
☐ Straighten up the area in which you will be hosting, put away clutter.	☐ Have ice for cold drinks. ☐ Set aside an area for coats. ☐ In the bathroom, leave out soaps and hand towels; put away personal items. *(Be sure to have a full roll of toilet paper to avoid an embarrassing moment for your guest!)*	☐ Have a pitcher of cold water in the refrigerator and cut lemon slices to put out for guests to use in their water or tea. ☐ Adjust the house temperature to a comfortable setting.
One hour before the meeting:	**Just prior to guests' arrival:**	**The doorbell rings:**
Relax ~ Get yourself ready!	☐ Turn on your house lights if needed. ☐ Set out foods. ☐ Have foods warming. ☐ Heat coffee and tea water.	Smile and greet your guests. ***It's book club time!***

:

If ever there was a book in need of a road trip it was this one. Got your interest?

Chapter 7

Field Trips: Take Your Club on the Road

Road trip, anyone? Kick it up a notch; field trips offer enrichment for your book club experience. Imagine visiting the author's muse, taking in the elements that caused he or she to put pen to paper. Reflect upon the author's choice of locality. What was it about the elements that inspired the author? Plan your field trip to evoke recollections of the book, its characters, and premise.

Creative Trips Make Fond Memories

While on a field trip, our club views each novel as having the potential to stir up memories of the pages read and the characters that gave the volume its life. Mostly we allow the novel to select the trip's location or the location, but on occasion, some locations help us choose the novel. Visit landmarks and other notable destinations in your own town or state, such as museums, outdoor parks, beaches, historic sites, or old school houses.

For further information, visit your state's Department of Tourism website or your town's Historical Register.

Organizing Trips

To ensure that everyone has a chance to provide input, schedule an organizational meeting. Be sure your members come prepared with their ideas and suggestions. As the ideas formulate, consider members' interests, capabilities, and economic situations. Unless one member likes to play travel agent (or one member absolutely does not), mix it up by allowing everyone a turn.

The time put into planning a field trip should be in proportion to the extent of the event. From the short day trip to the weekend getaway, field trips offer another instrument to navigating a book discussion.

After a tentative location is set, the planner should gather all pertinent details and reconvene the group for presentation and inquiries. The vote is in, the trips a go, now plans can be solidified. Succinctly, the date is booked, the destination secured, attendance confirmed, and rides arranged. Let the excitement begin!

As the outing approaches, it is important to communicate the trip's itinerary so everyone is prepared.

Ideally, trips should be planned in advance, but don't overlook that sudden opportunity to travel to a special event related to a book! The plans just need to be organized a little faster.

To assist in planning for future trips, it is helpful to keep a record (log) of all the suggestions, ventures and post trip comments. Take note of who organized and attended as well as the highs and lowlights. Use our "Organizer's Field Trip Checklist" located at the end of this chapter.

The following are some of our club's trip logs, anecdotes, adventures, and misadventures:

Lesson Learned – Keep Cell Phones Nearby!

On one of our excursions to a novel-based destination, we decided to stop for dinner on our way home. One member knew the perfect spot for fresh and tasty scallops; and, since we would not be back that way for the rest of the season, the stop seemed a no-brainer and everyone was excited. We were traveling in two separate cars; the group in the first car had put their purses in the trunk for better leg and seat room. That meant, unfortunately, that all their cell phones were now in the trunk! So, when the second group attempted to call and alert the first to the upcoming exit – the call went unanswered. Everyone in the second car began waving their arms and the driver was flashing the headlights – trying to get the first car's attention. The first car pulled over eventually, although by then we had missed the exit – and our chance to enjoy the "best scallops around." Instead, burgers became the "catch of the day" ... that was disappointing, but we made the most of it!

Trip Note: When traveling as a group, keep cell phones within reach of the passengers in every vehicle – or be sure Bluetooth or other hands-free devices are activated.

Trip Ideas and Locations

For years, our book club has enjoyed taking "book related" excursions together – and we encourage your club to do the same. We hope the following adventures can inspire your group to design an escapade of your own.

Winery Trip

Sue Grafton's novel, A is for Alibi, was the first book selection for our newly formed book club. When we reached our fifth anniversary date, the founding members decided to revisit that selection and plan a special trip to a local winery that featured a wine tasting bar, a fabulous view, and a beautiful open-air, covered porch (with outdoor heaters just in case of bad weather). The proprietor was generous, allowing us to bring snacks, and gave us plenty of time for reminiscing. To commemorate the event, we each received a keepsake copy of the book and each member autographed one another's copy.

The outing was a blast!

Have a backup plan in mind when the destination is outdoors in case of inclement weather. This way, members will be prepared to change plans quickly and the event will remain a success.

For more information on wine trails and vineyard tours in your state, visit www.winetrailsUSA.com.

One member was chatting with us about a concert she attended at Tanglewood, the summer home of the Boston Symphony Orchestra in Lenox, Massachusetts. This prompted us to hold our next meeting at an outdoor concert, which would perfectly integrate "novel to destination." This idea fit so well with our discussion of Daniel Mason's thought-provoking novel, *The Piano Tuner*.

An Indoor Outdoor Concert

The only thing predictable about the weather is its unpredictability! The trip date arrived and with it came torrential rain and the cancellation of the outdoor concert. Fortunately, the organizer had a back-up plan to salvage the meeting and theme. She transformed her living room into an "indoor music park," complete with blankets for comfort and room for our added accouterments. Settling in, we opened our lawn chairs, shared our hors d'oeuvres and toasted our host's ingenuity. The "concert" took form on a wide screen TV set to a symphonic channel, thereby deepening the ambience. Although Mother Nature had waylaid our originally planned trip, this back up plan saved the day. We enjoyed discussing a terrific novel – while attending a concert in comfort and dryness.

Trip note: We maintained all of the contact information in order to try this field trip at another time. In spite of it not being our original plan, this book club "adventure" ended up being one of the year's best!

Tuning in to a Book's Tone

The *Shadow of the Wind* by Carlos Ruiz Zafon begins with a memorable line: *"Welcome to the cemetery of forgotten books, Daniel."*

The creativity of Mr. Zafon is masterful. This narrative begs numerous questions: If it were up to you, what would the life span of the books on your shelf be? Which books would never again survive to have its pages turned? Conversely, which novel is worth fostering toward eternity?

Books, as with people and events only pass away when forgotten or left behind. This concept was rather intriguing and made for meaningful discussion, especially since *Shadow of the Wind* was our club's September read — and the exact date for the meeting was September 11, 2010.

Carrying forward the spirit of the book and the somber tones of that historic date, we choose to meet at Fort Hill Farm in the *"Quiet Corner"* of our state. Earlier in the year, we learned about this organic dairy farm run by a husband and wife team. The farm professed a tranquil pond and observation gazebo, glorious lavender fields set in the midst of dramatic rock gardens, and naturally, dairy cows. Upon our arrival, the farm's owner graciously gave us cover nestled amid the peaceful surroundings of lavender and stone. It seemed fitting to gather at such a natural and gentile setting to discuss the somber thoughts on our minds.

Trip Log: *Although this destination was not chosen for the book, the placid attitude of the surroundings was most fitting to honor such an historical day.*

Haunted Tour

October in New England is the perfect time for a book such as Ghost Stories of New England by Susan Smitten. The title and subject prompted us to participate in a tour of an historical graveyard and haunted house. Our guide entertained us with tales of local lore, complete with dinner at a purportedly haunted restaurant.

Whether you dine with a ghost or relish time spent in the home of a famed suspense author, planning a field trip during this month is hauntingly easy.

Off to the Races

Our original inspiration when we chose Seabiscuit by Laura Hillenbrand was to plan a trip to a horse race. Grand idea; however the track was too far for a day trip, requiring us to reconvene and reassemble our thoughts. After tossing around a few ideas, we found a fitting replacement: visiting a zoo in a nearby state. On the surface, a zoo has little in common with the story of Seabiscuit. Consider, however, that animals – in zoos or on the racetrack – live at the mercy of humans, and can live a life of respectful dignity or one of neglect and misery. The book follows the trials and tribulations of Seabiscuit's life, and illustrates the underlying saga of shameful human behavior – a fact that weighed heavy on our hearts. We researched ethical zoos and discovered the one we wanted to visit had an impeccable reputation for providing exceptional care to their animals. (Continued.)

So, on a cool overcast morning, we carpooled to this menagerie. As we walked among the animals' habitats, our chatter turned to discussing the book. To our amazement, other zoo visitors were joining our conversation! Two sweet ladies introduced themselves as members of a book club and were intrigued with the idea of going on a field trip with their members. We talked a while and exchanged a few book recommendations. Hopefully we influenced them to "hit the road" with their club members.

We then enjoyed lunch with a not-too-far-off view of a zebra, which was as close to a horse as we were going to get that day!

At the end of this entertaining and educational day, we trouped back to our cars with smiles and a sense of camaraderie one can only enjoy after a great book discussion.

Choosing Books that Lend Themselves to Field Trips

Below is a sampling from our past excursions which we hope will inspire you to organize a "novel destination" with your book club:

BOOK TITLE	AUTHOR	DESINATION
Life of Pi	Yann Martel	Indian Cultural Center tour
The Help	Cathryn Stockett	A day spa for manicures
Confessions of a Shopaholic	Sophie Kinsella	Dinner and shopping at the mall
Wicked	Gregory Maguire	See an off-Broadway play
The Old Man in the Sea	Ernest Hemingway	A dinner cruise

Organizer's Field Trip Checklist

Book that inspired the trip: _____

Destination _____

Address: _____

Web site: _____

Travel distance: _____

Tentative date(s): _____ Time: _____

Length of trip: _____

Meals: _____

Confirmed attendees and cell phone numbers:

_____

_____

_____

_____

_____

_____

On-site contact: _____

Phone: _____

Email address: _____

Date contacted: _____

Confirmation date: _____

Questions for On-Site Contact:

Is there a fee?   If yes, amount $ _____ Paid via credit card, cash or check (#): _____

Is a deposit required? If yes, amount $ _____ Paid via credit card, cash or check (#): _____

Reservation required? Yes: _____ No: _____ (Confirmation number _____)

Is there a minimum attendees? If yes, number: _____

Handicapped access? Yes: _____ No: _____

Hours of operation? _____

Inclement weather date (if applicable)? _____

Is there a meeting place for our group? _____

56

Catered/cafeteria/vending only: _____

Other: _____

_____

_____

Pre-Trip Checklist:

☐ Details sent to members (When? _____)

☐ Confirmed reservations

☐ Confirmed trip date: _____

☐ Departure point:

_____

☐ Exchange cell phone numbers (and keep cell phones easily accessible)!

After each trip, meet to discuss what worked and what could be modified to make the next field trip even better. Include suggestions here:

_____

_____

_____

_____

_____

Chapter 8

Young Readers and Teens Book Club

Realizing the need for children to be literate, many parents will introduce their toddler to picture storybooks then watch as that humble beginning grows into a young person's passion. By promoting this educational opportunity, young readers and teens can become skillful in the art of conversation, learning to formulate and clearly state opinion, and converse with their peers on a multitude of levels. Reading encourages a confidence that will last a lifetime.

Why Start a Children's Book Club

- Encourage good reading skills
- Provide an opportunity to enjoy a lifetime of reading
- Instill a sense of camaraderie throughout the group, and teach the basics of etiquette, sharing, companionship, and ownership
- Increase the amount of time a child spends reading
- Distract a child from the fast-paced world of technology and help them enjoy a slower, relaxed pastime, which allows them to exercise their minds
- Improve a child's attitude towards reading

  A child, who only reads what he/she "must" to pass a class, just might find excitement and enthusiasm in reading for fun

59

- Create an activity that parents can share with their child and his/her friends. This can be beneficial toward building strong family relationships.

How to Start

- Peruse the library or bookstore shelves to acclimate yourself to the books popular to young readers
- Visit your local children's librarian or teacher to help answer questions you may have
- Refer to the tools illustrated in this book

Let's Get Down to Basics

Each age group is unique. Most likely the young members will have preconceived ideas about who they would like in their club and what they would like to read.

They will need your guidance in:

- Deciding who to invite
- Finding a meeting place
- Maintaining an enthusiastic program
- Deciding what to read
- Keeping the club on track (nuts and bolts)

The Invite List

This may not be as difficult as you may think! Your daughter and her friends may be enthralled with the acclaimed *Junie B. Jones* series by Barbara Park. Your son and his pals may be sports enthusiasts. The friends who share these interests may be high on the list of invitees.

Or, you may choose to start a book club as part of an existing organization (such as a church youth group, library or community center). Ask the person in charge to help you get started and find interested young people.

An important consideration is the age level of your club. Younger children may be enthusiastic readers who could do well in a book club setting, but their attention span will be shorter. Be sure to structure meeting time and frequency appropriately.

Finding a Meeting Place

Look for an environment that offers comfort as well as an age-appropriate setting. You may need to take into account your participants' means of transportation. Will they be walkers, driven by an adult, or take a bus to the location? Consider any of the following options in your search for an appropriate site:

- Home
- Local library
- Community center
- School
- Church/synagogue, parish center, church school classroom
- Book store

Teens sometimes prefer bean bag chairs and a no-stress layout, while younger children may do better with sitting in a circle or other structured setting. Let the group's dynamics direct your decision.

Maintaining an Enthusiastic Program

An active, entertaining and "cool" club will keep participants coming back for more. In this age of immediate gratification, instant information and new technology, it may be a challenge to keep those young book clubbers' enthusiasm going strong over a period of time. The following tips may be beneficial:

- Listen carefully to each person's suggestions and notions regarding books, meetings, etc.

- Read the book they chose – you will be able to prompt the necessary leading questions

- Keep the focus on the members

  You may need to facilitate (although do not dictate), and always be prepared to be flexible!

- Respect each idea and opinion

- Come organized (and maintain control) with a solid agenda or schedule for each meeting

  Minimize downtime, which could be a catalyst for horseplay or boredom and make it tough to get the group back on track

- Be punctual and keep to the agreed length of the meeting

  Children will have homework and some older students may have a work or sports schedule

- Keep it challenging, but within their reading ability

- Insist on and maintain book club etiquette (see chapter 5)

- Do not dismiss the "dud" book choices. Discussions and commentaries on "why I didn't like it" may be just as much fun to chat about!

Remember that oftentimes adolescents may not yet have had the opportunity to voice their opinions or have an outlet to express their individual commentary on something they have read outside of the school setting. Once prompted, they may find a whole new world and discover a literary analysis never before revealed.

Do not forget to include yourself in the fun of this book club! You may have a favorite book or author from your younger days that you would like to share with the club. Try designating one meeting as the "Leader's Choice" for parents or other adult recommendations. Spice up the meeting by choosing a book that lends itself to a particular age-appropriate theme.

Naming the club is an excellent idea for an ice breaker! Help the young readers work together to come up with a name that embodies the uniqueness of the group, such as the "West Street Sleuths" or the "Razorback Readers." This will give ownership of the club to its members, and create a sense of camaraderie that is essential to a successful club.

Deciding What to Read

The choices of material can be overwhelming, especially for young readers. Look to the experts if you are not familiar with what is popular or would be a good read that will awaken their curiosity and promote plenty of discussion.

Look for books that have won awards or other designations as excellent indicators of well written books.

The Newbery Medal: The oldest and most prestigious award is presented annually by the American Library Association to a distinguished author of American literature for children.

- 2014 winner: *Flora & Ulysses: The Illuminated Adventures* by Kate DiCamillo
- 2013 winner: *The One and Only Ivan* by Katherine Applegate
- 2012 winner: *Dead End in Norvelt* by Jack Gantos
- 2011 winner: *Moon over Manifest* by Clare Vanderpool

The Caldecott Medal: Awarded annually by the American Library Association since 1938, this award is presented to the artist of the most distinguished American picture book for children.

- 2014 winner: *Locomotive*, written and illustrated by Brian Floca
- 2013 winner: *This Is Not My Hat*, written and illustrated by Jon Klassen
- 2012 winner: *A Ball for Daisy*, written and illustrated by Chris Raschka
- 2011 winner: *A Sick Day for Amos McGee*, illustrated by Erin E. Stead, written by Philip C. Stead

Coretta Scott King Award: This award is presented to authors and illustrators of African descent and promotes an understanding and appreciation of the 'American Dream.'

- 2012 Author Award: Kadir Nelson, author and illustrator of *Heart and Soul: The Story of America and African Americans*
- 2012 Illustrator Award: Shane W. Evans, illustrator of *Underground: Finding the Light to Freedom*
- 2011 Author Award: Rita William-Garci, author of *One Crazy Summer* (and a Newberry Honor book)
- 2011 Illustrator Award: Bryan Collier illustrator of *Dave the Potter: Artist, Poet, Slave*, (written by Laban Carrick Hill; also a Caldecott Honor book)

The Michael L. Printz Award: Annually, this award is given to a book which exemplifies excellence in young adult literature.

- 2014 winner: *Midwinterblood* by Marcus Sedgwick
- 2013 winner: *In Darkness* by Nick Lake
- 2012 winner: *Where Things Come Back* by John Corey Whaley
- 2011 winner: *Ship Breaker* by Paolo Bacigalupi

The Pura Belpré Award: This award was first presented in 1996 to honor a Latino/Latina writer and an illustrator who has published an outstanding work which commemorates the Latino culture in literature for children and youth.

- 2014 medal winner for illustration: *Niño Wrestles the World* by Yuyi Morales
- 2013 medal winner for narrative: *Aristotle and Dante Discover the Secrets of the Universe* by Benjamin Alire Sáenz
- 2013 medal winner for illustration: *Martín de Porres: The Rose in the Desert* illustrated by David Diaz, written by Gary D. Schmidt
- 2012 medal winner for narrative: *Under the Mesquite* by Guadalupe Garcia McCall
- 2012 medal winner for illustration: *Diego Rivera: His World and Ours*, by Duncan Tonatiuh
- 2011 medal winner for narrative: *The Dreamer,* by Pam Muñoz Ryan, illustrated by Peter Sís
- 2011 medal winner for illustration: *Grandma's Gift*, illustrated and written by Eric Velasquez

The Scott O'Dell Award: This award is in honor of Scott O'Dell, a renowned writer of historical fiction. To qualify, the book must be intended for young people or children and its story is placed in the United States, Canada, Central or South America. It also must be written in English by an American Citizen and published by an American publisher.

- 2014 winner*: Bo at Ballard Creek* by Kirkpatrick Hill
- 2013 winner: *Chickadee* by Louise Erdrich
- 2012 winner: *Dead End in Norvelt* by Jack Gantos
- 2011 winner*: One Crazy Summer* by Rita Williams-Garcia (also a Newbery Honor book and a Coretta Scott King winner)

Bram Stoker Awards: The Horror Writer's Association presented the first Bram Stoker Award for Superior Achievement in 1987. Named in honor of Bram Stoker, author of *Dracula*, the award recognizes outstanding work in the horror field.

- 2013 Young Adult Novel award winner: *Special Dead* by Patrick Freivald
- 2012 Young Adult Novel award winner: *The Diviners* by Libba Bray
- 2011 Young Adult Novel award winner: *Ghosts of Coronado Bay, A Maya Blair Mystery* by J. G. Faherty
- 2010 Young Adult Novel award winner: *Horns* by Joe Hill

Visit the websites for each of these awards to see lists of other books that were runners up, winners from past years or designations.

If the group decides to read a controversial book, we highly recommend informing the parents of the choice. Some parents may have religious or personal reasons for not wanting their child to read a particular book. Maintain positive communication with each member's parents and keep them a partner in this endeavor.

Keeping the Club on Track

This is the more formal aspect of running a club.

If you plan to have the meetings at a school, library, community center or church, ask about their building usage policy. Many localities will require forms to be completed and approved prior to your first meeting. Some places will require you to have permission forms with you at all times when using their property for meetings.

Ask parents to provide you with emergency numbers and to inform you of important medical information such as food allergies. This is especially important if your club will have a snack and if your group plans a field trip.

"Reading is a basic tool in the living of a good life."
~ Mortimer J. Adler

Chapter 9

Looking Beyond the Book ~ Giving Back

For several years, our book club has incorporated fun ways to challenge our membership while at the same time giving back to our local community – and we hope to inspire your book club to do the same.

Here's a quick look at some of our more memorable charitable efforts:

One year we decided to donate dolls to the local Toys for Tots program – but we wanted to make this an interesting and personal project. Prior to our November meeting each person drew the name of a fellow member from a hat, and then went out to shop for a doll that most represented the name that was drawn. At our meeting, we enthusiastically opened each unique doll and – working as a group – attempted to unravel the reasoning behind why it was purchased and who bought it. Knowing these sweet toys would make their way to needy children put us in the spirit of the holiday and brought our membership closer. This truly was an inspirational idea that made for a memorable holiday event.

Another year, we donated books to mothers and children living at a local women's shelter. To make it fun for our book club, we asked everyone to select books that characterize another member's unique taste. For us, the challenge was to choose a children's book and an adult book with the same member in mind. At our following meeting, we shared the stories of why the books were selected – which ranged from hilarious to sentimental. When we dropped off the books at the shelter, the director's eyes filled with tears. She explained she had been worried that the shelter would not have enough gifts for everyone at the next day's holiday party. Now, with our donation of books, that burden was gone. It was our honor to play a role in their holiday celebration.

Why volunteer? *You will gain as much if not more than you give!*
- *Share your skills*
- *Get to know your community*
- *Challenge yourself and others*
- *Make new friends and be supportive*

Looking Beyond the Book: Companions through Reading Partnership

Many members of the community – the elderly, the blind, developmentally disabled children and adults – would appreciate having someone to read to them. These "companion through reading partnerships" provide an opportunity for involvement, commitment, community, and service. Becoming a reading partner can be one of the most rewarding experiences for everyone in your book club (or just you, if you choose to go it alone). Books build bridges; reenergize readers, and change lives. So why not inspire someone in your community today?

Volunteering with people of any age, from senior communities to youth-oriented programs provides an important social outlet, intellectual activity, and can improve one's sense of self. For years, esteemed publications such as the *Journal of American Medical Association* have touted the virtues of reading as a brain-booster and age-fighter. Forming a reading partnership provides social interaction, prevents loneliness and lessens depression – important keys to a happy life.

Hopefully your club will join in the joy of giving back and helping others. If you desire to foster a "companion through reading" partnership, start by making a list of possible facilities or organizations that may be interested in this program, and then making an appointment to meet with the recreation director, facilitator or volunteer manager.

Questions to Ask

- Who is the main contact?

- Are assistants from the facility available to help with your reading partnership?

- How often could your group volunteer?

- What space or rooms are available?

- Are there personal or resident funds available to purchase books?

- Can you provide refreshments?

Now you can schedule a date and time to start your volunteer reading partnership. Pull together a list of books or other materials you would like the group to read, and get going!

You can organize a fundraiser to help the group purchase books, or you can start a book-borrowing program between facilities or the local library. Often times local groups such as the Lions, Rotary, and AARP clubs, or Boy Scouts and Girl Scouts are looking for local initiatives to support – and would love to know about your reading partnership program! Don't be afraid to write letters asking for support.

No matter where and when you ultimately decide to begin a reading partnership, the effort is well worth the time.

Check out the website www.volunteermatch.org for more ways to help your community.

We wish you the best of luck starting or jumpstarting your book club and would love to hear about your club's adventures, challenges, and inspirational volunteer experiences. Please share them with us at: colleymar@yahoo.com.

In an effort to promote a passion for reading, a portion of the proceeds from the sale of this book will be donated to community literacy programs.

Acknowledgements

Writing this workbook was an education in determination and stamina. If we can impart our best lesson, it is "hold fast to the dream, stay strong, keep the faith, and never give up on yourself."

Over the years, many people have influenced our journey but none more than our trusted guide, mentor, editor and friend – Kirstin Ahearn, to whom we are forever indebted. Her leadership, skill, inspiration and confidence in the future of this project were without exception.

Special recognition goes out to the efforts of Cindy Lubrico for her chapter reviews and unflappable faith in our venture. Our heartfelt appreciation goes out to our readers – Roberta McAloon, Ruth Reed, Sarah Hovic and Cheryl Ferraro – who gave of their time and effort in providing gentle yet honest critiques for each chapter.

Support comes in many ways and our best encouragers and cheerleaders were our families and friends. They provided a sounding board for all of our musings and quirky ideas, and watched patiently while we sat hunched over our computers working (or rushing out to yet another project meeting). Without them we would have long since given up! So to each of you we offer our love and thanks from the bottom of our hearts.

We would be remiss if we did not thank the members of the "Book and Beyond" book club ~ those past and present. Thanks to each and every one of you for helping to create one of the best book clubs ever!

~ S.C. and K.M.

Made in the USA
Las Vegas, NV
06 October 2022

56663244R00046